What is Scarcity of Resources?

Economics in Action

Jessica Cohn

Crabtree Publishing Company

www.crabtreebooks.com

Crabtree Publishing Company

www.crabtreebooks.com

Author: Jessica Cohn
Coordinating editor: Chester Fisher
Series editor: Scholastic Ventures
Editor: Amanda Bishop
Proofreaders: Adrianna Morganelli, Crystal Sikkens
Project coordinator: Robert Walker
Production coordinator: Katherine Kantor
Prepress technician: Katherine Kantor
Project manager: Santosh Vasudevan(Q2AMEDIA)
Art direction: Dibakar Acharjee (Q2AMEDIA)
Cover design: Ranjan Singh (Q2AMEDIA)
Design: Ruchi Sharma (Q2AMEDIA)
Photo research: Sakshi Saluja (Q2AMEDIA)

Photographs:
Alamy: Caro: p. 29;
  Iain Masterton: p. 6
AP images: John Bazemore: p. 13;
  Richard Drew: p. 11; Michel Euler: p. 7
Bigstockphoto: Gene_L: p. 8
Getty Images: Fred Ramage/Stringer: p. 26
Istockphoto: Chad Anderson: cover (center);
  Andresr: p. 17; Laughingmango: p. 12;
  Sean Locke: p. 19; Minten: p. 23; Nicolas
  Skaanild: p. 28
Jupiter Images: Brand X Pictures: p. 25;
  Creatas: p. 18; Hemera Technologies:
  p. 22; Don Mason: p. 10; Picturenet: p. 20
Q2A Media Art Bank: p. 5, 15, 16, 21, 24, 27
Shutterstock: Baloncici: cover (left); Natalia
  Bratslavsky: p. 4; Jaimie Duplass: p. 9;
  Christian Lagerek: p. 1, 14

Library and Archives Canada Cataloguing in Publication

Cohn, Jessica
   What is scarcity of resources? / Jessica Cohn.

(Economics in action)
Includes index.
ISBN 978-0-7787-4256-2 (bound).--ISBN 978-0-7787-4261-6 (pbk.)

   1. Economics--Juvenile literature. 2. Scarcity--Juvenile literature.
3. Supply and demand--Juvenile literature. 4. Capital--Juvenile
literature. 5. Natural resources--Juvenile literature. I. Title.
II. Series: Economics in action (St. Catherines, Ont.)

HB183.C64 2008   j330   C2008-903649-2

Library of Congress Cataloging-in-Publication Data

Cohn, Jessica.
   What is scarcity of resources? / Jessica Cohn.
      p. cm. -- (Economics in action)
   Includes index.
   ISBN-13: 978-0-7787-4261-6 (pbk. : alk. paper)
   ISBN-10: 0-7787-4261-X (pbk. : alk. paper)
   ISBN-13: 978-0-7787-4256-2 (reinforced library binding : alk. paper)
   ISBN-10: 0-7787-4256-3 (reinforced library binding : alk. paper)
   1. Economics--Juvenile literature. 2. Natural resources--Juvenile
literature. 3. Scarcity--Juvenile literature. 4. Capital--Juvenile literature.
I. Title. II. Series.

   HB183.C64 2009
   333.7'11--dc22

                                                            2008025372

Crabtree Publishing Company

www.crabtreebooks.com   1-800-387-7650

Published in Canada
Crabtree Publishing
616 Welland Ave.
St. Catharines, ON
L2M 5V6

Published in the United States
Crabtree Publishing
PMB16A
350 Fifth Ave., Suite 3308
New York, NY 10118

Published in the United Kingdom
Crabtree Publishing
White Cross Mills
High Town, Lancaster
LA1 4XS

Published in Australia
Crabtree Publishing
386 Mt. Alexander Rd.
Ascot Vale (Melbourne)
VIC 3032

Contents

Everything
Economics

Many people think **economics** is about money, and the flow of money is certainly a huge part of the economic picture. Yet the study of economics is much bigger than dollars and cents.

Making Choices

Economics measures what people will do as they make choices on how to use resources.

All people share Earth—its air, its water, its land, and the products and services its inhabitants produce. We sometimes struggle with sharing because we have competing needs.

Government officials debate what to do with reserves of rice. They set the price for a barrel of oil. They decide how to best direct the flow of money from bank to bank. This is part of economics.

So is deciding whether to use a $20 bill for a night out at the movies or a new T-shirt. Economics is the science of limited resources. Making choices about a resource, whether it is oil in the ground or money in your pocket, is central to this science.

▼ Billboards advertise products and **services** that businesses would like us to buy.

4

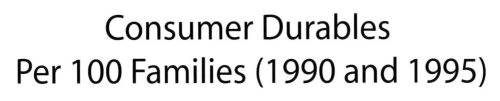

Consumer Durables
Per 100 Families (1990 and 1995)

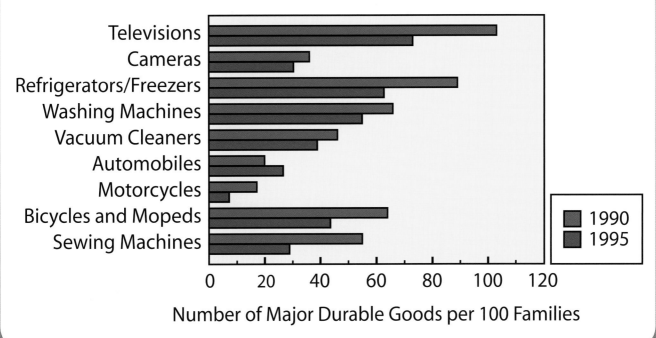

Televisions
Cameras
Refrigerators/Freezers
Washing Machines
Vacuum Cleaners
Automobiles
Motorcycles
Bicycles and Mopeds
Sewing Machines

0   20   40   60   80   100   120

1990
1995

Number of Major Durable Goods per 100 Families

▲ What did people have more of in 1990? In 1995?

Resources of all kinds combine to create **goods** and services. Goods are the things people want: automobiles for transport, food to eat, good-looking clothes. Services are actions that help satisfy people's needs and wants. Someone who looks after your health performs a service. A person who designs T-shirts does, too.

At any moment, people function as either producers or consumers of goods and services—or both. We participate in the economy even when sleeping; even our beds are goods. Economics touches everything.

FACT STOP

Living standard is a level of comfort, or wealth. In 1992, U.S. households averaged 1.6 televisions. Just ten years later, it was 2.1. Markers like these help economists judge living standards. Other markers include whether people own homes.

World of Needs

A person who wants something works for it, buys it, or both. Most people cannot produce all the goods and services they need. So trade or exchange is part of life.

▲ People in the silk market trade money for fabric they want.

Trading begins

Long ago, people traded one thing of value for something else of value: an animal skin for a spear or berries for firewood. People bought and sold by **barter**. Someone who made pottery could trade a bowl for flour. These are examples of **direct exchange**.

People then recognized that money could represent value. The people agreed that certain things, such as seashells, stood for an amount of worth. This became a **medium of exchange**. People no longer had to trade goods for goods. They traded money for goods instead.

▲ Irish musician Bono talks to economists at the World Economic Forum.

These days, people trade on paper or through computers. A bank might promise money to a business. They make an agreement on the forms that everyone signs. People participate in **indirect** trade when they use forms or papers and money instead of actual goods.

Economists study methods of buying and selling to see how they fit into these two larger systems of exchange:

- A **traditional market** is a competitive market. Sellers compete for customers. The price of goods and services sorts itself out.

- In a **command market**, a government controls the flow of goods and services.

Markets often mix both systems. In a lunchroom, for example, students might select offerings in a vending machine. The most popular brands "win." Yet school officials often have a say in which brands the school can sell and what the prices will be.

Going to the Source

When you put bills or coins into a vending machine, you are more likely to be thinking of hunger and thirst than connecting that action to national or world markets. Yet somebody owns the vending machine. Somebody made the snacks and beverages inside. Those connections and others link your decision to the outside world.

Production and Resources

Production is the process of turning resources into things that you and others want and need. **Productive resources** are materials and efforts used to produce goods and services. These resources can be divided into three basic groups: **natural resources**, **human resources**, and **capital resources**.

When you stand before a vending machine and select a box of crackers and a bottle of juice, you are using a bit of natural, human, and capital resources. How?

All Natural: To make the box, the cracker company needed cardboard, made from trees. Natural resources are all the things that come from Earth. Even the Sun is a natural resource.

▼ The timber on this land is a natural resource.

▲ This teen is a human resource in a clothing store.

People Power: Someone formed the juice bottle. Someone grew the fruit. Someone delivered the juice to the vending machine. Human resources include all the productive efforts of people.

Capital Idea: Then there are the capital resources, the items that humans make to use. The vending machine is capital. The school building it sits in is capital. What's more, the people who built that machine got training to be able to do so. The education they received for their jobs is another kind of capital.

All productive resources are limited. So it is important to use resources efficiently. Sometimes that means getting more from limited natural resources. Other times it means offering new training for workers. The economy "tells" businesses what to do.

FACT STOP

Producing more of anything, from clothing to college classes, requires labor, or workers. **Labor costs** include paying for workers, caring for workers, and training them. Labor costs are among the most expensive parts of production.

The Sky is the Limit

Productive resources are limited, especially the natural ones. Throughout the history of tree-rich North America, for instance, the lumber business boomed. Camps of lumberjacks opened. Towns developed. If trees ran out, the towns looked to other kinds of business or folded.

Other limits on resources

Human resources have limits, too. People have only so much time and effort to give. Businesses can increase worker output, or **productivity**. They can give workers better tools or technology to increase their output. Sometimes increases in productivity can lead to raises in wages and the standard of living.

▼ Limits on resources make some new cars hard to get.

Some limits on human resources are restricted to a certain point in time. There may be a shortage of auto mechanics in one decade because the number of trained mechanics falls short of **demand**. Yet people can be educated to fill those jobs in the future.

Capital is limited as well. Think about the car you hope to drive someday. There are only a certain number of them.

Improving physical capital like machinery can help with worker productivity. It can also put people out of work. Robots, for example, have replaced people on assembly lines. Those workers need to be retrained. So an increase in human capital can help bring back the balance.

The economy is driven by limits and how we address them. A car is worth more money than people tend to have. The car dealership might help arrange a loan for you. Adults can borrow to pay for goods and services, paying extra for the privilege of borrowing money. Borrowers must decide if a car is worth its price plus the extra money the loan costs. The money a bank lends out is another kind of capital—with limits.

The fact that you choose a certain car links you to other businesses and people. Bankers, for instance, watch to see which companies are profitable, and they invest in them. So the money you pay the bank ends up somewhere else. This is the nature of the economy. From limits come seemingly limitless possibilities for some kind of business growth.

FACT STOP

History celebrates people who became rich while helping others. One of those heroes is Bill Gates, a founder of the software company Microsoft. As a kid, he liked the game Risk, in which opponents overtake countries. As a man, he conquered markets and studies strategies for giving away his billions.

▶ Bill Gates helped found Microsoft Corporation.

Running Out

In boom times, there are plenty of resources and moneymaking opportunities to match. A good example is what happened in China at the start of the twenty-first century. Chinese officials started using some free market concepts. They produced and sold more of nearly everything—from toys to clothing.

What causes scarcity

When China opened markets and trade, there was rapid growth. Yet China, despite its rich landscape and large population, was soon dealing with scarcity. One huge problem was an oil shortage. The need for goods and services outstripped productive resources. Chinese officials started buying oil from other countries.

▼ Bad weather can ruin these crops for the entire season.

▲ Natural disasters like hurricanes can severely damage a community's economy.

Bad weather can ruin crops for a season. A storm can destroy businesses and homes. One group can start war with another. Technology can be outdated by better technology elsewhere.

Individuals are affected by these shifts in local, state, national, and international economies. If oranges have a bad season in Florida, people in North Dakota do not lose jobs over it, but the fruit becomes expensive.

One way to track the effects of scarcity is by **gross domestic product**, or GDP. That is the measure of a country's goods and services in a year. It shows how much activity people paid for. This works well in developed countries like Canada and the United States. It does not work as well in countries where there is a lot of farming and fewer goods to sell for money.

FACT STOP

Hurricane Katrina hit the U.S. in 2005. The levees in New Orleans, Louisiana, broke, and the area flooded. Power and clean water were wiped out in many parts. Roads and buildings were destroyed. At the five-year mark, that economy remained in ruins.

The Big Picture

GDP is measured in dollars in the United States and Canada. Economists either count all the money spent, or they can add up the income people made. To add the money spent, economists need to include money spent on consumption, money that was invested, money people sent to the government, and the balance of what was **exported** (or exports minus the **imports**).

What impacts the GDP

That's a huge number. A lot of things affect GDP. Because the number is so huge, many events will not make a dent in it. Bad times in one town where a plant closes down can be balanced by good times in a place where a mall opens up.

Larger factors, such as **inflation**, will register in the GDP. Inflation happens when money no longer buys as much as it once did.

Other times, there can be too much money flowing. People with money buy extras; demand goes up, and wages go up. Wages go up, and manufacturers raise prices. Inflation also happens when things are scarce, as they are during war. When there is inflation, people tend to stop buying as much as they did in better times.

When economic activity falls too low, the country is said to be in **recession**. If you think of the economy as a healthy young person, inflation is a high fever, and recession is when that person gets sick and goes to the hospital.

▼ People with too much extra money can drive up costs of shipping and wages.

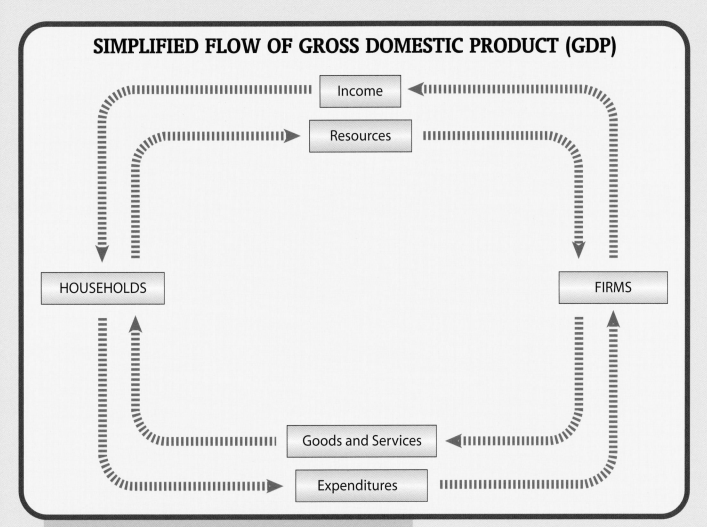

SIMPLIFIED FLOW OF GROSS DOMESTIC PRODUCT (GDP)

Income

Resources

HOUSEHOLDS

FIRMS

Goods and Services

Expenditures

▲ What flows opposite to the flow of resources and goods? The payment in dollars! Imagine if there was a break in any part of the flow. What would happen?

The federal economists figure out what is ailing the economy and how to respond.

Macroeconomics is the branch of economics that deals with that big picture. Goods and services are produced by either businesses or the government or through the cooperation of both. Businesses build ships, but government builds bridges. In macroeconomics, economists look at the economy as a whole and consider factors with big effects. They concentrate on ways governments can affect downturns in the overall economy.

FACT STOP

To cure recession, economists change the money **supply**. They pump more money into the market and hope the cost for borrowing falls, so more people borrow more money.

The Individual's View

One branch of economics centers on government policies. Yet another branch is about how individuals and firms act and react. One affects the other in major and minor ways.

Individuals are predictable

Individuals make decisions, trying to get the most from their incomes. Businesses make choices that will bring the most profits. You might think that individuals make unique choices; each person is different and special. You might think that businesses are all so different that they must behave uniquely. Yet if you study enough people and enough businesses, you see some of the same things happen over and over.

What happens over and over? Prices rise too far. If resources needed to make your favorite shoes become scarce, the price will go up. You might pay the price for a while, but at some point you might wonder if other shoes might be worth a try.

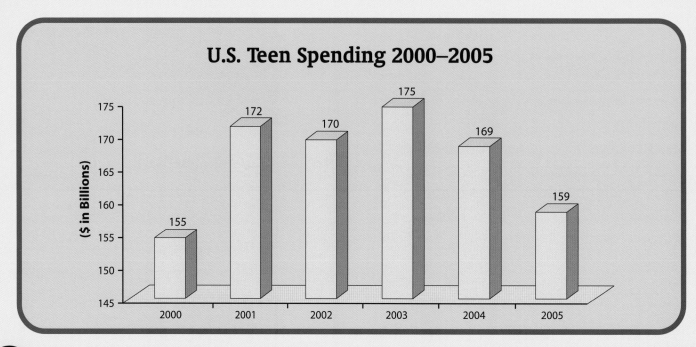

U.S. Teen Spending 2000–2005

▲ People make decisions about how to spend their money.

At a sale, you might stock up on a certain shirt, while it is on sale knowing the price is rising. You might end up with so many shirts that they are not special anymore. This is known as **diminishing returns**. People want something until diminishing returns convince them otherwise.

Another thing you can count on is that people will make some wild decisions. People make bad decisions when they are missing information. Wild decisions fall under a category of behavior economists call irrational behavior.

Let's say one movie theater offers tickets a dollar less than elsewhere. But the theater is 20 miles away. By the time you get there, you have spent your savings on gas. That is irrational.

Microeconomics centers on these ideas. In this branch of economics, economists look at why people make financial decisions. They look at why businesses behave in certain ways. They pay attention to supply and demand.

FACT STOP

Keep track of where money goes over a month. Look for holes! Another great habit is investing in yourself. Do you get an allowance? Do you earn money from chores or a job? If you put aside $10 a week, you have $520 after a year. Double that for over $1,000.

Supplying a Reason

Whether you look through the lens of macroeconomics or microeconomics, the price of business and the cost of happiness keep changing. Prices affect individual and business behavior immediately and directly.

One high price brings another

If oil costs rise, transportation costs do as well. So the price of delivered goods goes up. Oil products are used to make plastics, too. Higher oil costs can even affect the price of the packaging of those goods.

Changes in supply or demand lead to price changes. When flat-screen TVs first arrived, for instance, manufacturers had to work out how best to make them. The big ones were thousands of dollars each. They were sold to people able to pay to be first to own the technology. But soon, more units were produced, other technology surpassed it, and prices fell.

Producers of goods—and services—make the most of times when prices are high. Higher prices encourage increases in production. Demand helps determine the level of output in a market. But increases in production can also decrease raw supplies. So it is a balancing act—which sometimes becomes a need to reinvent the product.

▼ When oil supplies are low, the cost of plastics goes up.

We adjust to less supplies

Car manufacturers, for example, deal with ever-smaller gas supplies. So they are producing cars that run on less gas. In an age when anyone can get information from the other side of the world in a split second, people no longer think in terms of just their homes, their blocks, or their family circles. In a world where scientists are spreading alarms about pollution and the limited nature of natural resources, vehicle manufacturers search for newer, cleaner ways to produce the power to run cars.

Supplying anything is going to cost something. You have to pay for productive resources. You have to pay for the people involved. With any product, the cost of supply keeps going up. People who run businesses keep watching the price of supplying each unit of their product or service. If it reaches a point when they must raise prices, they do. If the market no longer supports their product, they either fix the product or get out of the market.

FACT STOP

When music became available on the Internet, it became harder to convince people to buy CDs. Before then, some CD prices were close to $30.

▶ Buying an item online means paying for a web service, packaging, shipping, gas for the delivery, and the item, too.

Demanding
an Answer

Let's say someone wears a certain hat, and the look catches on. The hat is sold at a local shop. The shop sells out of the item. The next week there are more hats, but the price has gone up. Demand drops. When an economist talks about demand, he or she is talking about the price people want to pay, can pay, and do pay for something.

▲ When a clothing trend hits, demand can be high.

Other effects of demand

Or maybe demand does not drop. Instead, the look catches on elsewhere. The company that makes the hat starts to deal with cotton shortages. The price goes up all over. Yet people pay the extra!

Manufacturers and other business owners keep an eye on demand, supply, and price. They review production to keep up with demand. They lower supply costs when they can and prices as needed to produce even more demand. They stay mindful of income levels among the people they are trying to reach.

Having **competition** encourages businesses to do their best. They not only produce what consumers want, they tend to produce goods and services for the lowest cost. Competition encourages efficiency.

Let's say one company makes cell phones. It operates in a country with a high standard of living. The workers earn good wages and benefits. Then a company in a country with a lower standard of living starts making cell phones that work as well, for half the price.

Owners of the first company can increase demand with successful advertising. But the cost of advertising might then increase the price further. Do they branch into another business? Do they lower the price by searching for new suppliers or by cutting into profit? Do they make deals with other countries to make sure theirs are the only phones that get imported? Sometimes the answer is "all of the above."

You may think it is not fair to be in business and lose out to a business with lower operating costs—especially in another country. Yet competition tends to make everybody in competition better. In the case of the cell phone companies, the people who need cell phones can benefit.

FACT STOP

Let's say a new video game system is invented. The price can be set as low as $250. That is a lot of money, but not as costly as other systems like it. The company surveys customers and comes up with these numbers. Should they raise the price?

▼ Does the graph indicate that the game system should sell for more than $250?

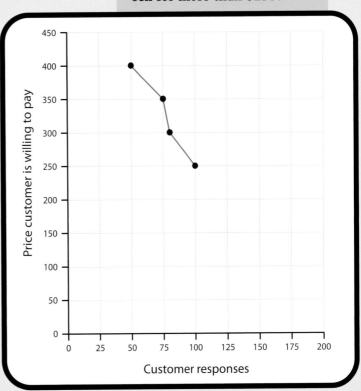

Price customer is willing to pay

Customer responses

21

Making a Choice

Supply. Demand. Price. These are economic building blocks. Yet there is one basic impulse that informs them all: choice. The choices that consumers make, as groups or as individuals, drive the markets.

How do you choose?

TV shows sell advertising to make money. Yet too much advertising can turn people off. Viewers can choose among shows. They can even choose shows with no advertising, paying extra for those. Sometimes the best choice is taking one service from one provider and another from yet another provider. In that case, the viewer will allocate money between two services.

▲ A restaurant's opportunity cost may be the item that does not make it on the menu.

The runner-up among the services is called the **opportunity cost**. Why? The viewer gives up that opportunity for the first choice. You might not think about your second choices much, but businesses do!

Businesses have opportunity costs as well. They survey their resources and decide how they will best use them. The second-best choice is their opportunity cost.

▲ How do you choose whether to watch a certain show or station? What is your opportunity cost?

When making these choices, people consider **tradeoffs**. If a restaurant chef thinks about raising prices for steak, he or she is going to look at the possible loss of demand for steak. So there is an **incentive** to consider all possible outcomes. An incentive is a reward or penalty that influences decisions.

The choices people make can be determined by scarcity. Let's say someone wants to have dinner out. He or she has a limited income; money is scarce, after all. When dining, one possible incentive might be having a gift card for the restaurant. That savings may help the diner choose.

Scarcity makes choice necessary from the start. Whether they think about those limits or not, they zero in on a way to be as happy as possible.

FACT STOP

Authors like Malcolm Gladwell explain how economics is a way to understand people. In his book *Blink: The Power of Thinking Without Thinking*, Gladwell says that a trained mind makes choices in a blink. Someone will zero in on opportunity costs as if by instinct.

The Happiness Factor

Economics boils down to being happy with your choices. Resources are scarce. Even choices can be limited. Yet happiness is the final product most people value.

How choices make people happy

Businesses are happy when making as much profit as possible. A person is happy when getting the most from the market. In both cases, the way to make the most of opportunities is measuring the **utility** of your choices and taking measure of opportunity costs. Measuring the utility of something can be as simple as ranking it.

Perhaps your family enjoyed visiting a store to pick movies to rent. You were limited by the choices the store had made. Next, you tried ordering movies from a cable or satellite company. Maybe you got tired of that because you became limited by the company's choices. Then you found you could order just about any movie ever made— from a mail subscription. The movie-rental company made it easy for you by providing return envelopes for your DVDs and by being fast with replies.

▼ If you saved just $50 a month and put the money in the bank, you would have over $70,000 in 40 years!

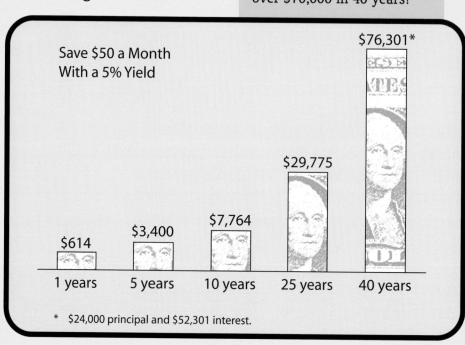

Save $50 a Month
With a 5% Yield

$76,301*

$29,775

$7,764

$3,400

$614

1 years   5 years   10 years   25 years   40 years

* $24,000 principal and $52,301 interest.

24

Yet consider the fact that choosing a DVD supplier is affected by your entertainment budget. If you enjoy watching movies and also adding to your music collection, you might need to portion money between those two. So one opportunity cost might be feeling you are giving up too much of your music download budget for your movie supply.

Utility can seem to drive a hard bargain: everyone goes after what he or she wants. It can make it seem as though people get the most from utility at all costs. Yet people use input from their hearts when they make decisions as well. One of your opportunity costs may be the point when you think you are hurting other people with your choices. Part of what you demand might be the feeling that you are helpful to people beyond yourself.

FACT STOP

Griffin wants a new guitar. He earns $70 a week. His first–choice guitar costs $1,100. If he saves $30 a week, he can have the guitar in 36 weeks. His second-choice guitar is $800. Griffin starts saving for his first choice. But he knows he can take the second choice and still accomplish his goal.

Ending Poverty

Getting and spending are not the start and end of economics. Economists also study the flow of resources and human behavior to figure out the biggest problems of our time.

Economics and the poor

Among the biggest challenges is poverty. The 2000 U.S. Census revealed that poverty in New York City had grown by ten percent during the previous decade. Poverty increased even more dramatically for people who had been in the city for more than a decade.

One-fifth of New Yorkers lived in poverty four years later. Poverty was defined as having a third of the money and things that people generally had. While economists define poverty with numbers, poverty has a more immediate meaning for those who suffer from it. For the poor, it means not going to the doctor when a doctor is needed. It means skipping meals.

This large U.S. city might seem to be unique. But poverty is everywhere. About 980 million people live on $1 or less a day. The people surviving on that little cannot afford any kind of jolt—from bad weather, political drama, or anything else. They are holding on by a thread.

▶ People living in poverty often do not have money to buy food.

Around the world, women and their children make up the majority of these poor. From country to country, there are many standards for poverty, but starvation and lack of shelter are sure signs that should not be ignored. Forty thousand children die each day from hunger or hunger-related illness. A world food shortage threatens peace on the globe.

So how do people make the most of scarce resources to meet demand with supply for basics like food, water, and health care? While some people starve, food goes to waste elsewhere. Can governments provide incentives for other governments to cooperate?

Economists continue working toward these goals by studying and explaining what works and what does not work when humans deal with scarce resources.

▼ One in four U.S. children now lives below the poverty line. Economists often refer to the poor in wealthy countries as the "hidden poor."

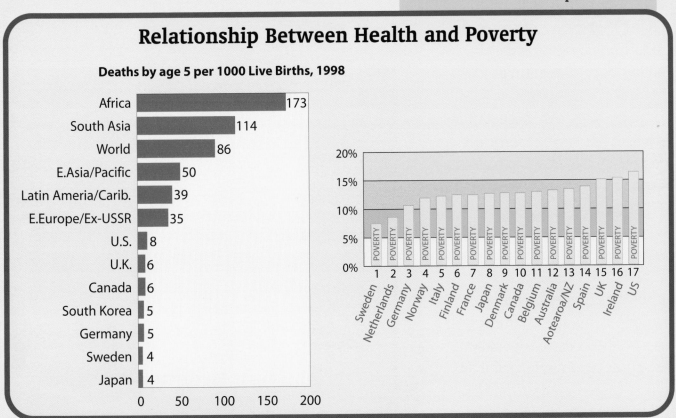

Relationship Between Health and Poverty

Deaths by age 5 per 1000 Live Births, 1998

Africa	173
South Asia	114
World	86
E.Asia/Pacific	50
Latin Ameria/Carib.	39
E.Europe/Ex-USSR	35
U.S.	8
U.K.	6
Canada	6
South Korea	5
Germany	5
Sweden	4
Japan	4

Countries (1–17): Sweden, Netherlands, Germany, Norway, Italy, Finland, France, Japan, Denmark, Canada, Belgium, Australia, Aotearoa/NZ, Spain, UK, Ireland, US

Green
Lean Earth

Economists often point to the **distribution of wealth**. That is a comparison of wealth across groups. Economists and others look at the distribution of wealth around the globe.

Making the most of our resources

Wealth does not refer to money flowing toward someone or something. So someone who makes half as much money as someone else can be wealthier than that person by making better decisions. The same goes for nations.

Some historians say geography has determined much of the world's wealth distribution. Having waterways to control trade contributes to wealth. Having natural resources like iron ore does, too. But as the economy becomes more global and as trade widens, officials look for new and better ways of using and sharing resources.

Governments are responsible for the defense of their nations. They make markets as competitive as possible, while looking after natural resources and the environment. The successful government makes these changes as long as benefits outweigh costs.

▼ Windmills and solar panels are good for Earth and the economy.

So what happens when natural resources are used, polluted, or destroyed? What happens when people are not educated for jobs that are needed?

Scarcity is a challenge of these times for all nations. Global warming has been recognized since the 1880s, but dramatic weather events in recent years have acted like an alarm. Caring for the environment is looking smarter all the time.

Oil production may peak any day now. So we look for ways to power production other than with gas. Scientists and engineers try to come up with new inventions and processes. It will take many solutions, some small and some enormous. It will also take new thinking, informed by an understanding of how the economy works.

FACT STOP

In 1999, Allan Durning wrote a book called *Green Collar Jobs*, about the struggle to balance concerns for business and the environment. These days government officials talk about the possibility of using "green jobs" to grow the economy.

▼ Governments may develop "green jobs" like installing solar panels.

Glossary

barter Trade of goods without an exchange of payment

capital resource Human-made thing used for production

command market Economy in which government controls flow of goods and services

competition Contest for scarce resources, goods, and services

demand Desire and ability to gain something; also, the supply of that thing

diminishing return Point when using resources toward something yields no gain

direct exchange Simple trade without need for other payment; barter

distribution of wealth Comparison of wealth across groups

economics Science of limited resources

export Something sold in another country or the act of doing so

goods Things people want

gross domestic product (GDP) Measure of country's goods and services in a year

human resource Productive effort of people

import Something brought into a country for sale or the act of doing so

incentive A positive or negative that gets people or things to do something

indirect Trade exchange done using money or promises of some value

inflation When money no longer buys as much as it did

labor cost Includes pay, caring, and cost of education for workers

living standard Level of comfort or wealth

macroeconomics The study of financial relationships as a whole thing

medium of exchange Something accepted as having a certain value, used in trade

microeconomics Study of behavior of units of the economy, such as companies or households

natural resource Thing needed for production, which comes from Earth

opportunity cost In decision-making, the cost of passing up the next best choice

productive resource Capital, human, or natural resource used in production

productivity The efficiency of production

recession When the output of an economy falls for a period of time

service Action that helps satisfy people's wants and needs

supply Goods or services on the market

tradeoff Benefit given up when making a choice

traditional market Competition in which sellers compete for buyers

utility Satisfaction of consuming a good or a service

Index

Webfinder

http://www.yourmoney.cba.ca/tsam/en/tsam/
http://www.younginvestor.com/
http://www.frbsf.org/education/fedville
http://www.themint.org/
http://www.pbs4549.org/economics/index.htm
http://www.socialstudiesforkids.com/articles/economics/scarcityandchoices1.htm

Printed in the U.S.A.